The Wonderful Workings of God for His Church and People

by Samuel Bolton
with chapters by C. Matthew McMahon

Copyright Information

The Wonderful Workings of God for His Church and People, by Samuel Bolton, with chapters by C. Matthew McMahon Edited by Therese B. McMahon

Published by Puritan Publications
A Ministry of A Puritan's Mind ®
Crossville, TN
www.puritanpublications.com
www.apuritansmind.com

Manufactured in the United States of America 2022.

eISBN: 978-1-62663-432-9
ISBN: 978-1-62663-433-6

Table of Contents

God's Wonders Among His People
by C. Matthew McMahon, Ph.D., Th.D.

"Declare his glory among the heathen, his wonders among all people," (Psa. 96:3).

The church of Jesus Christ is to declare the glory of God among the nations (*i.e.* heathen and people). The glory of God can be seen in the covenant of redemption (God's eternal covenant between the Father and Son to Redeem his people) and the covenant of grace (the covenant of redemption seen in time and history working out among the people God will save). God's glory is only *clearly* seen by those who have been redeemed in such a glorious covenant and by the Mediator, Jesus Christ. That does not mean those who are *without excuse* cannot see the invisible attributes and divine power of God (Romans 1). They can. But where God's glorious presence in redemption is concerned, only those saved and redeemed are able to experience the glory of God in Christ for their benefit. 1 Corinthians 2:14 says, "But the natural man does not receive the things of the Spirit of God, for they are foolishness to him; nor can he know them for they are spiritually discerned." And Romans 8:8, "...the carnal mind is at enmity against God, for it is not subject to the law of God, nor indeed can be. So then, those who are in the flesh, cannot please God." In order to rightly understand God's *glory*, men must understand first that God exists, that men are sinners and that Christ is the sole Mediator who is able to saves sinners. The heathen nations, in having the glory of God declared to them (Psalm 96), must first see that 1) God exists, 2) that they are wicked, and 3) that *God* must save them. Such a proclamation of the good news of the Gospel is the word of truth they need given to them by the life and witness of believers. Do not talk to them merely concerning sanctification, but of the cross. Do not talk to them concerning angels, but the cross. Do not talk to them concerning spiritual songs, but declare the glory of God in the cross of Christ; for the glory of God is manifested predominantly *in the cross*. The glory of God is seen in all perfection in Jesus Christ and his sacrifice. Express God's glorious perfection of redemption seen in the cross of Jesus to them. Through Christ, and the presence of the church, (that means you as a believer), the holiness of God is *now* manifested. His glory is expressed by his people as an outlet in their praise.

The church is not only given the command to declare his glory, but also, "his wonders." This refers to the wonderful, historical achievements that God has accomplished in and through his people. The word *wonder* here refers to things that are unusual and have a connotation of things *God works*. How unusual are they in terms of things God works for us? God came down from heaven, was born and conceived of a virgin by the power of the Spirit, lived a human life and then was killed for preaching the truth of God, raised himself on the third day and then ascended into heaven, so that he may send forth his Spirit to dwell in the hearts of believers so that on the final day he may raise up to everlasting life all those who believed on him through the power of the Holy Spirit. This is *wonderful* and uniquely *unusual*. This is what we proclaim, what we look back to, and this is what David in this psalm proclaimed, what he looked forward to in the coming Messiah (*cf.* Genesis 3:15). This is a public sharing of the Messiah based on what God has done in the midst of his people, not just private musing.

The function of God's *wonders* is for God's glory. But it is also to make mercy available to the recipient and not only to be a demonstration of his power. God is not simply shooting off fireworks to show how great he is. He *already knows* intimately how glorious he is and how glorious all that he does is for his glory and for his name's sake. But interestingly, he desires us to *declare this great work* so that *we* may be used by him as a vessel to bring the good news of the gospel to the ends of the earth and to know his glory *ourselves*. In fact, we are to express it in such a way that we do so in the light and clarity of heathen nations. And we know, since we live after the time of the coming of the Messiah, that the wonders of God are seen in the redemption of Jesus Christ *now accomplished*. It is the wonder of the cross, the wonder of his death, the wonder of the redeeming power held in them, and the wonder of the blood which so *wonderfully* cleanses us from all sin for the glory of God. The Apostles were immediately sent by Christ to preach the gospel to the whole world because it was God's demonstration of his *wonder*. This is what Paul did, "But we preach Christ crucified," (1 Cor. 1:23).

The church is not simply to declare his *glory*, but also his *wonders*, not just to the heathen, but, "among all the peoples." This repetition reminds us of our Gospel duty. A more specific translation here in the psalm is, "together with all the peoples."[1] Its connotation is that we are coming together with all the people of the world to sing and declare God's glory and wonders in praise. It is a longing for the fellowship of all nations together under Christ. When Adam was in Eden, he walked with God. Then he disobeyed and fell from grace and glory. Within the bounds of the new covenant and salvation echoed in Genesis 3:15 and brought to realization in Christ, after the fall God walks with man once again. There should be a *yearning* to gather in all the peoples of God into the community of the faithful to have his wonders declared among them. Who but the carnal man can refuse to tell the truth of God's wondrous grace and Christ's eternal love?

---

[1] See my work, *Psalm 96: A Theology of Praise*, Second Edition, for a full study on this topic.

It is our duty to *understand* God's glory and his wonders, and to make *known* his glory *and* his wonders. This is what we live for! But to declare it we must understand it, and to understand it compels us to declare it, for we cannot hold our tongues back to testify to the glory of God, those who truly are partakers of his glorious grace which is found in no one else than Jesus Christ. Our view should be a world-wide domination of the Gospel over the peoples of the earth to bring them into the fold of the Good Shepherd. In this, all the earth is to share in the wonders of God's glory.

This is the substance of what Bolton will explain in detail, and will demonstrate as he considers the wonderful workings of God to his church and people from Exodus 15:11, "Who is like unto thee, O LORD, among the gods? who is like thee, glorious in holiness, fearful in praises, *doing wonders?*"

In His Grace,
C. Matthew McMahon, Ph.D., Th.D.
From my study, March, 2022

Meet Samuel Bolton

by C. Matthew McMahon, Ph.D., Th.D.

Samuel Bolton, D.D. (1606-1654), divine and scholar, who has been wrongly identified both with a son and a brother of Robert Bolton, B.D., was born in London in 1606, and educated at Christ's College, Cambridge.[2] In 1643 he was chosen one of the Westminster Assembly of divines. It is stated that he was successively minister of St. Martin's, Ludgate Street, of St. Saviour's, Southwark, and of St. Andrew's, Holborn. He was appointed, on the death of Dr. Bainbrigge in 1646, master of Christ's College, Cambridge, and served as vice-chancellor of the university in 1651. Although with "no ministerial charge"

---

[2] Le Neve, *Fasti*, ed. Hanly, iii. 690, 607.

he "preached gratuitously every Lord's day for many years." It is believed that it was this Samuel Bolton who, in 1648, attended the Earl of Holland upon the scaffold.[3] He died, after a long illness on October 15, 1654. In his will he gave orders that he was to be "interred as a private Christian, and not with the outward pomp of a doctor; because he hoped to rise in the day of judgment and appear before God, not as a doctor, but as a humble Christian." Dr. Edmund Calamy preached his funeral sermon.

His works are *rare*. They are:

1. "A Tossed Ship making for a Safe Harbor; or a Word in Season to a Sinking Kingdom," 1644.
2. "A Vindication of the Rights of the Law and the Liberties of Grace," 1646.
3. "The Arraignment of Error," 1646.
4. "The Sinfulness of Sin," 1646.
5. "The Guard of the Tree of Life," 1647.*
6. "The Wedding Garment," and posthumously,
7. "The Dead Saint speaking to Saints and Sinners," which is a series of works in one volume: (a) Sin The Greatest Evil, (b) A Treatise of the Loves of Christ To His Spouse,*[4] (c) A Treatise of the Nature and Royalties of Faith, (d) A Treatise of the Slowness of Heart to Believe, (e) A Treatise of the Miserable Condition of

---

[3] Whitelocke, *Mem.* p. 387.
[4] * = republished works by Puritan Publications.

Unbelievers, (f) A Treatise of the Wonderful Workings of God For His Church and People.[5]

For Further Study:

Brook's *Puritans*, iii. 223-4; Clark's *Lives*, pt. i. 43-7; Calamy's *Funeral Sermon*, 1654; Bolton's *Genealogical and Biographical*, Abram's *Blackburn*, p. 264.

---

[5] *A Treatise of the Wonderful Workings of God for His Church and People*, by Samuel Bolton, D.D. and Master of C.C.C. (London: Robert Ibbitson, 1656). Exodus 15:11, "Who is like unto thee, O Lord, amongst the gods! who is like thee, glorious in Holiness! fearful in Praises! — Doing wonders!"

Part 1: The Text Explained

"Who is like unto thee, O LORD, among the gods? who is like thee, glorious in holiness, fearful in praises, doing wonders?" (Exodus 15:11).

When troubles threaten us, God charges us with two things: 1. The first thing in God's charge is faith. Psalm 55:22, "Cast thy burden upon the Lord," the burden of fears, of cares, of troubles. There is the charge; and the discharge follows, "and he shall sustain thee."

2. The second thing God charges us with is prayer. Psalm 50:15, "Call upon me." But if you will take the charge and the discharge together, see Phil. 4:6, "Be careful for nothing," there is the discharge. "But in all things make your request known to God," there is the charge.

And there are two practices God charges us with when fears invade us: 1. Thankfulness. 2. Obedience. The former you read in Psalm 50:15; the latter in 1 Sam. 12:24. Thankfulness and obedience have been the practice of the saints when they face calamities and troubles, coupled with faith and prayer.

In Esther's time when God delivered his people, they responded by praising him. The same was true with the early Christians who observed days of prayer for the removal of the pressures on them. In addition, they observed their solemn feasts and times of praises when God delivered them.

The lack of mercy sends us to prayer; the enjoyment of mercy sends us to praises. This was the practice of Moses.

Exodus 14 tells of Moses' dangers and fears when the Egyptians pursued him, verses 8-10. And in the middle of this difficulty, you see his faith in verses 13-14, and then the 15th verse implies his prayer. The Lord said to Moses, "wherefore do you cry unto me? Speak unto the children of Israel, that they go forward." By this response from God, it is implied that Moses' spirit wrestled mightily with God in prayer, though the words he uttered are not recorded.

Later in this chapter you read of his praises for that great deliverance which God brought them. No sooner was he come to shore, but he sings forth the praises of God, both for their own deliverance and the enemy's destruction.

These words are part of a psalm of thanksgiving for the glorious and wonderful deliverance of the children of Israel from the armies of Pharaoh.

Everything is summarized in verses 9-11. There you read of these three things: 1. Man's purposing. 2. God's disposing. 3. The church's retribution.

Man's purposing in verse 9. The enemy said, "I will pursue. I will overtake. I will divide the spoil. I will draw my sword and my hand shall destroy them." And in the thoughts of the Israelites, the Egyptians had already destroyed them.

We have God disposing of the Egyptians in the next verse, "The sea covered them: and they sank as lead in the mighty waters." And *then:*

The church's retribution, by way of admiration of God's excellencies, "who is like unto thee, O Lord among the gods! Who is like unto thee, glorious in holiness! Fearful in praises! Doing wonders!" Here the church is riding in triumph, in a majestic solemnity, admiring God and triumphing in him, as she still does in all her songs of praises for deliverances (see both Judges 5 and 1 Samuel 2). Also consider Isaiah 25:9, "Lo, this is our God: we have waited for him, and he will save us: this is the Lord, we have waited for him, and we will be glad and rejoice in his salvation."

Now let's continue to the doctrine.

Part 2: The Doctrine

The doctrine drawn from these passages is this: our wonderful God does wonderful things for his church and people.

God does not only do *wonders*, but *great wonders* (Ps. 136:4). No, *mighty wonders* (Dan. 4:3). He does amazing, astonishing wonders for his church and his people.

In the execution of this doctrine, we will go through these five points. We will show you: 1. The truth, that God does wonders. 2. The ground and reason, why God does such wonders. 3. What those wonders are which God does. 4. When God does these wonders. 5. Whether God will do a wonder for us.

1. For the first of these, God does great wonders for his church, even such things as are above our thoughts, above our hopes, above our expectations, above our reason to conceive, and above our faith to believe.

The whole scriptures are but the *annals* or *records* of the wonders which God has done for his church and people. You can all tell me what wonders God did for his people in Egypt. The psalmist tells you in Psalm 78:12, "Marvelous things did he for them, in the sight of their fathers, in the land of Egypt." And you know what wonders he did for them at the Red Sea, when there was nothing but death before them and death behind them;

they were surrounded by death. Yet then God unbared his arm and caused the Red Sea to divide itself. It became a passage for the one and a grave for the other.

He also did wonders for them in the wilderness. Not a day without a wonder; every day was the birth of a wonder. He gave them bread from heaven and water out of the rock. Read the 78th Psalm and the 9th chapter of Nehemiah at your leisure, and in them you shall see a chronicle of the great wonders which God did for his church and people.

But now to the doctrine that God does wonders for his church and people.

God has wonderfully disrupted great plots and desperate counsels and created designs against them.

We will give you an instance of this in Haman's time. Haman had a desperate plot for the ruin of the church and people of God (Esther 8-10). In brief, his plan was to overthrow and put to death all the Jews on the pretense that they did not keep the king's laws.

The means by which this design was shattered was *the hand of God*. To begin with, the king could not sleep well. So, he got up from his bed and retrieved a book, the book of chronicles. And surely guided by providence, he opens and reads that passage concerning Mordechai and his faithfulness in discovering and disrupting a murder intended against the king. Whereupon God set this act of faithfulness so close to the king's heart that he could not rest until Mordechai was rewarded for it. And this reward was Haman's ruin. His advancement was Haman's abasement.

Another example is found in Daniel 6:4-5. The nobles wanted to ruin Daniel who was faithful to the king, and yet they could find no way to ensnare him apart from something that concerned the law of his God.

Therefore, their plot was to make a decree that whoever should ask any petition either of God or man for the space of thirty days, except from the king, would be thrown into the den of lions.

And, of course, the plot worked according to their desire. For notwithstanding this decree, Daniel continued to make his regular prayers and supplications to God three times a day, as you see in verses 10 and 11.

As soon as this happens, they go and tell the king: "Have you not, oh king, made a decree that none should ask any petition of God or man, except of you? There is one Daniel of the captivity, who does not regard you, oh king, nor the decree you have signed, but makes his supplication three times a day," (verse 13).

Though Daniel was a better subject than the best of them, they demonstrated him to be rebellious to the king simply because he was obedient to his God.

But God disrupted their plan and brought their own plot to their ruin, as Daniel was preserved by the lions that should have destroyed him.

2. God brought wonderful deliverance for his church. Weakness and strength are all one with God, as Asa confessed when that great army came against him.

"It is all one with you, to help with many or with few," (2 Chron. 14:11). Infinite wisdom and power know no difference. No means can be so contemptible that he cannot use them to his own purposes.

The greatest means will be no privilege without God's blessing; likewise, the smallest means shall be no disadvantage if God blesses them. God sometimes armed natural causes as the sun, moon, stars, hail, and wind against the enemies of the church. The stars in their course were said to fight against Sisera. The Lord slew the enemies of Joshua with hail and the Moabites with the sun shining upon the water.

And we read in ecclesiastical history that the Christians, when fighting against the barbarians, were in great distress for lack of water. They prayed to God, and he sent them an abundance of rain to refresh their army while meeting their enemies with thunder and fire from heaven. In remembrance of this experience, the Romans called the Christian legion "the thundering legion."

Sometimes God chooses to infuse his strength into weak and contemptible means for the deliverance of his church. For example, Cyrus was, compared to most, a weak prince. And yet God used him to overthrow the strongest people in the world, the Babylonians, and by him to deliver his church. Deborah was a woman, and yet God raised her up for the deliverance of his church (Judges 4 and 5).

2. Sometimes God works the deliverance of his church without any means at all, and this is even *more* wonderful. When God looks about and sees there is no man, when the stream of second causes is dried up, then God himself stands up for the defense and deliverance of his church and people and creates deliverance out of nothing.

What God does by means, he can also do alone. What he does intermediately, he sometimes does immediately from himself. For example, the angel killed one hundred fourscore and five thousand *immediately* (2 Kings 19:35).

History tells us that when Julian went to war against the Persians, he vowed to his idol gods that when he returned, he would offer a sacrifice of all the Christians in the empire. And yet God undertook the deliverance of his people himself, smiting Julian from heaven with an unknown blow, and by that saved his church.

Further examples include Maximus and Herod (Acts 12:23). Though there may be weakness below, yet there is strength above. And when means are lacking, God will create means, or he will work without them.

3. Sometimes God works the deliverance of his church by contrary means. And this is yet a more wonderful way.

God often brings good out of evil, life out of death, *etc.* As the physician orders poisons and destructive ingredients to physical, useful, and healthful purposes, so those things which in themselves are against us, God in his singular wisdom and mercy turns them for us. That which has been used as the means of ruin, God often turns to the means of raising a church and a people.

This is like the opening of the blind man's eyes with clay. One would think it should rather put out the eyes of a seeing man than give sight to a blind man. But if Christ is doing the work, though the means seem ever so contrary, they shall be effectual.

Thus, you see that God often does wonders for the good of his church and people.

Part 3: The Grounds and Reasons for God to Do Wonders for His People

We come now to the second thing: the grounds and reasons.

1. The first of which is because he is a wonderful God. Wonderful things befit a wonderful God. His *name* is wonderful (Isa. 9:6), therefore, his works are wonderful. This is the inference noted in Psalm 86:10, "You are great, and do wonderful things." Great enterprises, great difficulties, great accomplishments befit great spirits. And wonderful works befit a wonderful God.

And upon this ground God's working may not be demonstrated until the time is desperate, because that is when we may better discover his great power. Such deliverances are most suitable to our great God. He could as well have saved Lazarus from sickness as have raised him from the grave: but he allowed him to die, be buried, and lie three days in the grave that he might magnify his power in raising him to life again. He lets the difficulty go beyond the help of man, that you might better know what the power of God is.

2. The second reason God does wonderful things for his people is to get himself a wonderful name, that God might be known in the world. This is one of the reasons God executed such dreadful judgments on

pharaoh, and brought about such great deliverances for his people, to show the greatness of his name and his power to the known world (Isa. 63:12). Special cures win more glory to the physician than a thousand ordinary cures. So special victories win more honor to a general than a thousand ordinary skirmishes. And so here, special deliverances bring God more glory than a multitude of ordinary occurrences.

If God should only walk in the ordinary ways of his providence in the world, his glory would not be seen and advanced. Therefore, God often steps out of his ordinary paths of providence, and goes in extraordinary directions, that he might show forth his glory and power and advance his own name.

Know this, that it is God's great design in the world to advance his own name and make it glorious to the ends of the earth. And one way God accomplishes his purpose is by doing *wonderful* things for his church. In this way, God wins a great deal of honor and praise from the saints as well as dread and terror from the wicked.

You know how terrible the name of the God of Israel was to all the earth because of the great wonders God did for Israel while they were in Egypt.

This, therefore, was the argument David used for why God should destroy his enemies and bring about deliverances for his people, that men might know, "that Thou, whose name alone is Jehovah, art the most high over all the earth," (Ps. 83:18).

Great mercies and wonderful deliverances demonstrate the wonder and greatness of God, something that smaller events cannot do.

Great deliverances show his great power, great mercy, great wisdom, and great truth. God is lost in smaller deliverances but very visible in those greater ones. They who are unwilling to acknowledge God in lesser situations are forced to acknowledge him in greater deliverances; and to say with them, "the finger of God is here."

None but God could have disrupted such counsels. None but God could have discovered such plots. None but God could have removed such evils. None but God could have wrought such deliverances.

3. The third reason God does wonderful things for his church is to *uphold* his great name. An illustration of this truth is found in Deuteronomy 32:27. God was highly displeased with Israel for their provocations of him; and he threatened to destroy them. Yet after all this, he said, "I would scatter them into corners, and would make the remembrance of them to cease from among men: were it not that I feared the wrath of the enemy: lest their adversaries should behave themselves strangely, and lest they should say, our high hand, and not the Lord, hath done all this."

The same situation is noted in 2 Kings 18:35, "Who are there among the gods of the countries, that can deliver out of my hand?" This was the argument which Moses urged God with when the Lord threatened to destroy the children of Israel, "Now if thou kill this people, then the nations which have heard the fame of thee, will speak, saying: because the Lord was not able to bring this people into the land, which he swore unto them, therefore hath he slain them in the wilderness," (Num. 14:15). It is as if Moses was saying, "You have gotten yourself a name by the mighty wonders which you have done for your people. If you choose to leave now and do no more, you would lose the glory which you have gained, and the nations would be ready to charge you with weakness and impotency because you were not able to do what you promised and purposed to do for your people."

Similar instances can be found in Deut. 9:28 and Exodus 32:12. And in Joshua 8:9, when God allowed the armies of Israel to be smitten by their enemies, Joshua said, "O Lord, if it be thus, what will become of thy great name?"

These arguments arose from the necessity for God to do great things for his people in order to uphold that great name he had gotten, which otherwise would be dispelled. As Psalm 79:9 says, "Help us, for the glory of thy name; and deliver us for thy name's sake." And Isa. 48:9-11, "For my name's sake will I defer my wrath, and for my praise will I refrain it from you, that I do not cut you off."

4. God does wonderful things for his people, that he might *receive* wonderful praises from his people. Therefore, God works wonderful deliverances for his

church that his church might return praises to God again, "He has done his wonderful works to be remembered," (Ps. 111:4). It is as if he had said it was for this end: that God did those wonderful works, brought about those great deliverances, that they might be remembered, "that they might be kept upon the imagination of the thoughts of the heart forever," (1 Chron. 29:18), that we might be *living monuments* of thankfulness, trumpets that sound forth the praise of his greatness and goodness, from generation to generation. He that forgets thankfulness, forgets the end of God's bestowing of mercy, robs himself of the fruit and effect of the present mercy, and hinders himself of future blessings.

5. God does wonderful things for his church to add torture to the devil *and* the devil's children. God's mercies and deliverances to the saints enrages the devil and wicked men. When Haman prevailed to get a bloody decree against the Jews, he rejoiced as one that promised to himself the utter ruin of them all. But then God stepped in to disrupt his design, and how much this added to Haman's torture and vexation.

God has his ways to make wicked men gnash their teeth before they even come to hell; and this is one way he does it. He puts this hope in their heart, "I will pursue, I will destroy, I will divide the spoil." And then he suddenly turns it all upside down, blowing up their projects, bringing all their enterprises to nothing, which ends up vexing and torturing their souls!

6. God does wonderful things for his church and people that both us and the generations to come might be quickened and stirred up to trust in him and obey him.

1) That we might be quickened to trust in him. This was the fruit of that great deliverance in the text, "And Israel saw that great work, which the Lord had done upon the Egyptians: and the people feared the Lord, and believed the Lord," (Exod. 14:31). According to David, "God that hath delivered me from the lion and the bear, he will also deliver me from this uncircumcised philistine." And Psalm 63:7, "Because thou hast been my helper, under the shadow of thy wings I will rejoice." That is, "because you have been my helper, I have had experience of your goodness to me in such and such straits. Therefore, under the shadow of your wings I will rejoice. I will not only trust in you, but rejoice, being assured you will help me in time to come."

Men that are not mindful of former experiences, still seek help in every fresh difficulty. But where experiences are the premises, assurance may be the conclusion.

David was a man of many choice experiences of God's goodness to him, and he laid them up and made use of them at every need. He did not only make use of the experiences themselves, but of everything that was a part of it or a trophy of it.

When he was forced to flee from Saul, coming to Abimelech the priest, he requested a weapon from him for his defense and safeguard. He told him there was none, except for the sword of Goliath whom he had slain. And David said, "There is none like that, give it to me," (1 Sam. 21:9). This was a trophy of God's goodness to him. It was a symbol of a former experience of God's love to him, and there was no better weapon for his defense than this which was *both* an experience and a weapon. In carrying this sword, he also carried an experience with him which could also comfort and encourage him.

In 2 Corinthians 1:10, the Apostle Paul said, "he has delivered us from so great a death and does deliver: in whom we trust he will yet deliver us." From his former experiences of God's goodness to him, Paul creates an argument of future deliverances.

If we were wise enough to treasure up former experiences, these former aspects of our lives would come in to help the latter; and the longer we live, the richer in faith we should be.

We ought to trust God, though we had never tried him. But when he helps our faith by former experiences, this should indeed strengthen our confidence and make us to go to God as to a tried and trusted friend.

If we were well read in the history of our lives, we might have a bible of our own, drawn from the experiences of God's dealings with us. This way we should be able to say in any difficulty and distress, "I dare trust God in this difficulty and this present distress.

I have tried him and found him true. He never failed me. And because he has been my help, therefore under the shadow of his wings will I rejoice." This is the first part of the reason God does wonders, to enlighten and encourage his church and people to trust in him and obey him.

2) God also does wonderful things for his church and people that the generations to come might be encouraged to trust in the same God in like distresses.

The church made use of former experiences, as shown in Psalm 22:4-5, "Our fathers trusted in thee: they trusted, and thou didst deliver them: they cried unto thee, and were delivered: they trusted in thee, and were not confounded." And from this the church gathers an argument that God who delivered others would also deliver them.

In Isaiah 51:9-10 the prophet says, "Awake, awake, put on strength, O arm of the Lord: awake, as in the ancient days, in the generations of old. Are you not he that wounded the dragon? Who dried up the sea and made the depths a way for the ransomed to pass over?" It is as if he had said all those former experiences of God's gracious dealings and wonderful deliverances of his church are all encouragements to us, to believe his goodness to us. And therefore, the psalmist tells us in Psalm 9:10, "They that know thy name will trust in thee," and then he gives the reason – "for thou Lord hast not forsaken them that seek thee." He does not say, "thou

Lord will not," but, "thou Lord *has not*." God's has-not is his will-not too.

Men may change, men may alter their mind. But God does not. Men may repent of former behaviors. Or they may resolve to do no more. But God does not change his ways. He will not forsake his people.

He will be gracious because he has been gracious. God's former dealings towards his church and people inform us as to what his future behavior shall be to his church and people. He has not forsaken us; therefore, he will not forsake us.

Even those times when God temporary pulled his protection from his people Israel, it was because they were living in direct disobedience to his commands. He performed great and miraculous works for them, and yet they did not believe him.

Part 4: God's Loving Engagements to His People

7. God will do wonderful things for his church because of his *covenantal* love.

There are four loving engagements of God which move him to do wonderful things for his church:

1) *They are his people.*

2) *His promises to them.*

3) *His people trust in him.*

4) *They seek him for refuge.*

1) God is engaged to do wonderful things for us because we are his. We are his people, and he is our God. We are his spouse and he, our husband. We are his children and he, our father. We are his members and he, our head. We are his portion, his inheritance, *etc.*

This is a great engagement for God to do great things for us. What will a loving father not do for his child? What will a loving husband not do for his wife? We stand in these same relationships with God.

He thought nothing was too much to suffer for us. He suffered great things, and he suffered cheerfully; he was in tormenting pain until the hour of his death came. Do you believe that he would now think anything was too much to do for you?

God does whatever is accomplished in the world. And there is nothing that he does, that I may say his heart is more in or that he does with more delight, than those things he does for his church and people. His whole heart is in them and for them; and therefore, everything he does for them he does cheerfully and fully. As you know, whatever your heart is in, you do willingly, you do thoroughly, *etc.*

Indeed, there was nothing to engage him to make us his people. Before he made us his people, as Moses said, "God chose you, not because of your righteousness, or the uprightness of your heart; for you are a stiff-necked people." Rather, it was because the Lord loved you.

But there is something to engage him; something to do for us now. He made us his people. And because we are his people, "The Lord will not forsake his people, for his great name's sake, (1 Sam. 12:22). And why? What is the reason? What is the engagement? "... because it has pleased the Lord to make you his people."

2) A second loving engagement which causes God to do wonders for his people is because of his many great and precious promises. God's promises are engagements upon himself. God made himself our debtor, not by receiving anything from us, but by promising all things to us.

He has made promises of preservation, as in Isaiah 33:16, "He shall dwell on high: his place of defense shall be the munition of rocks; bread shall be given to him; his waters shall be sure."

I know of no more full and complete promise in Scripture in which all objections that a fearful heart might raise are answered and taken away. Let us look at this promise more closely.

a) He shall dwell on high. If he were among his enemies, he might be in danger. But the fact that God dwells on high, or rather on "heights," (as the word is more correctly translated), meaning many ascents, many heights, above the reach of danger, out of range.

b) But suppose they could raise up mounts and come as high as he was. They still could not hurt him for he is in a place of defense.

c) But surely his defense is not so strong that it cannot be broken through. And yet the text says that is impossible, for his place of defense shall be the munitions of rocks; many rocks; and many munitions of rocks (and therefore impregnable) to guard him.

d) But he may be starved out; his supply will not always last. There is no plowing and sowing on rocks; he will eventually starve. And yet the text says bread shall be given him; he shall be provided for.

e) But what shall he do for water? There is no water to be had out of rocks. This very thing is what challenged the faith of Moses, to fetch water out of a rock. And yet the text here says, he shall have water too.

f) But his water may run out. It will not always last. And yet the text says his waters shall be sure and shall never fail.

Again, in the same chapter, verse 21. "The Lord will be to us a place of broad rivers and streams, wherein shall go no gally with oars, nor shall gallant ship pass thereby," clearly shows the defense God would provide to his people. He will be a river between us and our enemies. But not only a river; he will be a broad river, a river that cannot be passed over. "... a river, wherein no gally with oars shall pass."

But may a ship pass? No, no ship shall pass for the Lord is our judge; the Lord is our lawgiver; the Lord is our king; he will save us. But what if any ship should attempt to cross over? You see in verse 23 what God will do, "Your tackling is loosed; they could not well strengthen their mast; they could not spread the sail."

2. And as he has made promises of preservation, he has made promises of deliverance out of trouble. As Psalm 34:19 says, "Many are the troubles of the righteous; but the Lord delivered him out of them all." And Psalm 50:15, "Call upon me in the time of trouble; I will deliver thee." And Psalm 91:15, "I will be with him in trouble, and will deliver him." And Isaiah 54:17, "No weapon formed against him shall prosper."

That love which moved him to make these precious promises to us will never give him rest until he makes good on those promises.

3. A third loving engagement which causes God to do wonders for his people is because they trust in him. Trust is a kind of engagement upon a man, although he has made no promise. A man will not deceive another who puts his whole trust in him, even if he is not engaged by promise. There is a kind of engagement in trust itself. Shall we then think that God would be any

different, when he has made so many precious promises to us? If God should call us away from other shelters and tell us that if we will trust in him, he will be our refuge and our security, and then he should fail to fulfill his promise, this would be the greatest deceit in the world.

No, my brethren, there was never a man who put his confidence in God who did not find God to be everything to him which he expected.

Faith engages all the power, all the wisdom, all the mercy and truth of God to help us. And if the power, wisdom, *etc.*, of God can do wonders for you, then God will do wonders for you if you believe in him. Believe (said Christ) and you shall see the wondrous works of God.

4. A fourth engagement, which causes God to do wonders for his people is because they seek him. He does not say to the seed of Jacob, "seek me" in vain. He has styled himself as the God who hears prayers. He bids us call upon him in the day of trouble, and he will hear. The prayers of God's people are so many engagements upon God, to move him to do for them. Faith and prayer will set God to work. It will set the power, wisdom, and mercy of God to work for you. Faith and prayer will move mountains. Nothing shall be too hard for that people whose hearts and spirits God upholds to believe and to pray.

There is a kind of omnipotence in faith and prayer, because these two companions set the omnipotent God, as well as the omnipotence of the power of the omnipotent God, to work for us.

Part 5: What are the Wonders God Will Do?

Thirdly, what are these wonders which God does for his church and people?

1) God does wonders for the *souls* of his people.
2) God does wonders for the *body* and outward man.

He does wonders for the soul. The first wonder, and indeed the wonder of wonders which God has done for his church and people, is the giving of Christ for us and to us. All wonders are swallowed up in this wonder: God manifested in the flesh. Therefore the Apostle Paul says in 1 Tim. 3:16, "Great is the mystery of godliness," God manifested in the flesh. That such greatness and such meanness, such finiteness and such infiniteness, such riches and such poverty, such strength and such weakness, so great a God, and so lowly a man, all in one. This is a wonder.

There are four great wonders found in this, as well as a wonder of humility which will appear if you consider who he was and what he became.

1) Consider who he was. Christ was the Son of God, the express image of his Father, equal with God. And yet he thought it not robbery to be equal with God; he was God blessed forever.

2) Consider what he became. He did not take on the nature of angels but rather the nature of man, subject

to infirmities. And what a wonder of humility was this? The maker of the earth, to be made of earth.

Then there was a wonder of wisdom. That God should create such a way to redeem us when we were lost. The combined consultations of men and angels could never have found a way to both reconcile God's mercy in the salvation of man and satisfy his justice in the damnation of sin.

It is as if God said, "You are miserable creatures, but I am a merciful God. The demands of my justice I cannot deny. Neither will I deny the entreaties of my mercy. Find me then one who can satisfy my justice, and I will show my mercy to you." Ah! Where could we have found one strong enough to bear sin and to satisfy the wrath of God for us? It took the wisdom of God to find the way. This wonder of wisdom we adore and admire.

Here also was a wonder of love. A height, a depth, a length, a breadth... a love beyond all dimensions. This is a love beyond knowledge, a love that may be apprehended by faith and yet not comprehended by reason. It was an infinite love. Christ, who understood the greatness of it, said in John 3:16, "God *so* loved the world [so infinitely, so incomprehensibly], that he gave his only begotten son, that, whosoever believes in him should not perish, but have everlasting life."

There was a wonder of mercy as well, which will be more conspicuous if we consider first the person, and then the time.

1. The person who undertook this redemptive act was the second person in the glorious trinity. It is the person against whom the first sin was in some respect committed. He is the wisdom of the Father and called Wisdom (Prov. 8). And the sin of Adam was against this wisdom, to be *like* God. Therefore, the greater wonder of mercy is that he against whom the first sin was committed should undertake its expiation.

2. Consider the time when he took on our nature. And that was when we were brought to a desperate loss. The time when it was evident that nothing else could help us, "Sacrifice and burnt offerings, thou wouldst not have," (Heb. 10:6-7). When legal washings were declared insufficient to pay for our sins or to accomplish our peace with God, then Christ comes into the world. Christ did not come into the world until it was made evident, that without him God could not be satisfied, nor man be saved. And so, this is the first wonder: the sending of Christ in whom all is wonderful. His incarnation, the hypostatic union of two natures in one person, his passion, resurrection, ascension, session, intercession; these are a chain of holy wonders. Therefore, Christ is called *wonderful* in Isaiah 9:6 because everything regarding Christ and his redemptive work is wonderful.

1) He is wonderful in his person and natures: equally both God and man, equally both mortal and immortal, finite and infinite, so great, and yet so lowly, so rich and yet so poor. This is a wonder.

2) He is wonderful in his offices of king, priest, and prophet.

3) He is wonderful in his government.

That he should bring us to life by his death, to glory by his misery, to honor by his shame. All these are wonders.

Another wonder God does for the souls of his people is the work of conversion and regeneration. That a man should partake of another begetting, of another birth, of another nature than others in the world and even than he himself had, this is a wonder. That a man should be the same, and not the same: the same man bodily, yet as different in qualities as if another soul lived in the same body. That he should live by another life, be fed by other food, refreshed by other comforts than others are. Here is a wonder, that a spirited lion should become as gentle as a lamb, or a Saul become Paul, a persecutor become a preacher. This is a wonder.

And even greater is the wonder if you look upon the weak and contemptible nature of the means God uses to work his wonders through – that of a weak man. It would have been no great wonder if the walls of Jericho had fallen because of the battery of a canon. But this made it the wonder, that the blast of ram's horns should bring down the walls of Jericho. And this is what makes this work more wonderful, that by such weak and contemptible means and men this great work should be effected.

It is like when a man comes into the church full of pride, lifting up his head, ranting at God, glorying in his sin and shame, and even perhaps coming with the explicit purpose to condemn and scorn the minister. To see this same man then return home because of the ministry of a weak man, crying out with shame, "God be merciful to me a sinner," or with Paul, "Lord, what will you have me to do? I am willing to do anything, to suffer anything," *etc.* Here is a wonder.

And as the birth of a Christian, so the life of a Christian in grace is wonderful. It is a mysterious life, a life hid from the world. For the source and spring of this life is secret and mysterious. Its nourishment is mysterious, and its conveyance of nourishment is mysterious.

When God holds up a man's heart to fear him, to seek him, to believe in him in times of darkness and temptations, here is a wonder. All the workings of faith are wonders, but especially in temptations and desertions.

That a man by faith should conquer a troop of fears, silence an army of doubts, answer a throng of disputes and carnal reasonings, overcome all the powers of darkness to chase ten thousand devils before him which all the power of earth cannot do, here is a wonder.

That a man by faith should hold up his head under the burden and guilt of many thousands of sins, the least of which would sink the soul, here is a wonder.

That a man by faith should be a rock in the midst
of a storm and stand immoveable when the winds blow
and the billows rage and when heaven and earth seem to
come together, as described in Psalm 46:1-3, "I will not
fear, though the earth be removed, though the
mountains be hurled into the midst of the sea," this is a
wonder.

When God shall keep alive a little spark of grace
amid a sea of corruptions, hold up his own work amid all
counter-workings, oppositions of sin and Satan, here is
a wonder.

When God makes a man willing to sacrifice his
goods, liberty, and even life itself rather than wound his
conscience and offend his God, this is a wonder which,
without the power of God could not be wrought.

When God shall bear up the spirits of the saints
with joy and comfort, in the absence of all created
comforts, as you see in Habakkuk 3:17, "Although the fig
tree shall not blossom, nor shall fruit be in the vine, yet I
will rejoice in the Lord, I will joy in the God of my
salvation."

In the presence of all difficulties, to stand up and
rejoice under the frowns, menaces, scorns, scourges,
prisons, and persecutions of men, to embrace the stake,
kiss the chains, smile on the terrors of death, rejoice with
Stephen under a shower of stones, these are wonders.

When God turns all the afflictions and even all
the sins of his church and people to the good of his
people, to humble them more, to strengthen their faith

through the exercise of prayer, and to make them more watchful, these are wonders.

Secondly, God works wonders for the outward condition of the church.

God often restrains the wickedness and malice of men against his church, such that even though they are full of evil and fury, they are unable to wield any harm against the church and people of God.

This was true of Rabshakeh. When he came with purpose to destroy Jerusalem, God restrained him (2 Kings 19:28-33). This made David say, when the princes counseled together to take away his life, "my times are in thy hands," (Ps. 31:15). Though they are full of malice, they shall not be able to hurt me. They could not act against me for God restrained them.

God has the devil and his wicked men in a chain; and they cannot go a jot further than he allows, and that shall be no further than for his own glory and the good of his church, as he tells us in Psalm 76:10, "Surely the wrath of man shall turn to thy praise, and the remainder of wrath shalt thou restrain."

Though wicked men may be full of wrath against the church, God will not allow them to hurt his people. And this is a great wonder. He sets boundaries on the fury of men as he does to the raging of the sea. He not only puts boundaries around them, but he also calms and stills them.

You see this with Esau whose revengeful rage and desire to kill his brother Jacob was calmed by God.

So instead of killing him, he falls upon his neck and kisses him. God caused this change of heart in Esau. And therefore, it is said in Genesis 33:10 that, Jacob saw the face of Esau as the face of God. It was not Esau, but *God* that he saw in Esau's face. He saw God appearing in the wonderful changing and calming of his spirit, who came with such fury against him. And this was the fruit of his wrestling and praying the night before.

When God carries out his purposes with weak and contemptible power, when he makes weak means accomplish great purposes and effects, this is a great wonder. It is a wonder that God does often, as you see in 2 Chron. 14:11, "And Asa cried unto the Lord his God, and said, Lord, it is nothing with thee to help, whether with many, or with them that have no power: help us, O Lord our God; for we rest on thee, and in thy name we go against this multitude. O Lord, thou art our God; let no man prevail against thee." As the mariner can turn about the greatest ship with the smallest rudder, so God, who sits at the helm of his world to steer and govern all, can bring about his own purposes by the weakest means. God brought Jeremiah out of the dungeon with old rotten rags that were good for nothing, so he makes use of such means in times of difficulty for the deliverance of his church.

As God weakens those he intends not to prosper, so he strengthens and guides with a spirit of wisdom those he intends for the deliverance of his church. You see this in Deborah and in Cyrus, who though he was a weak prince, God used him to overthrow the strongest people in the world at the time.

When God makes the afflictions and persecutions of his church a means for growth and increase of his church, this is a wonder. As was said of the Israelites in Exodus 1:12, the more they were afflicted, the more they grew. And God has done the same for his church. History recounts thousands who were brought into the body of Christ not by sermons but by the sufferings of his saints. The blood of those martyrs served as seed to propagate his church.

And Julian knew this so well that he stopped persecuting the church as his predecessors had done, not out of mercy, but envy (according to the historian), because he saw that the more they were afflicted, the more they grew; the more they were oppressed, the more they increased.

When God brings about the peace of his people by their troubles, their healing by their wounding, their comforts by their fears ... when God works to bring joy out of sorrow, life out of death, create comfort out of discomforts, this is a wonder. These wonders God frequently shows for the good of his church.

And how often has God made the lusts of men, and even the malice and rage of his enemies, to be a means for the good of his church and people? He turns those things which would naturally have been for their ruin a means to raise and elevate his church and people.

The narratives of Pharaoh, Haman, and others afford us with plenty proof. Out of those things which are destructive in themselves, God brings comfort and deliverance. This is to show that only God can turn poison into food, evil into good. God turns the evil of sin and trouble to the good of his church. As it was in the waters of Bethesda, the waters were troubled before the diseased were healed. God made the trouble of the water subservient to the cure in the water. Likewise, he often makes the troubles of his people subservient to the growth and increase of his people.

The whale which swallowed up Jonah, God made a means to bring him to the shore. And that trouble which we think will swallow us up, God makes to advance our peace here until he sets us upon the shore of eternity.

We ourselves have had the experience of it. But this is the Lord's doing, and it is wonderful in our eyes.

When there seems to be nothing but thoughts and preparations for war and destruction, God shall be pleased to compose our differences, heal our breaches, change the sad face of things, and beat our swords into plowshares and our spears into pruning hooks. This is a wonder.

And this is a wonder which only God can do, a wonder which he has done, a wonder which we have had experience of, and such as we are now in expectation of, which God may in his mercy grant.

Part 6: When Does God Do Great Wonders for His Church?

When does God do these wonders for his church? When he shall gain the most glory from the enemies of his church and people. This is when God does his wonders.

God often delays acting until his enemies have dug graves to bury themselves in and twisted cords to bind themselves with, so that their confusion might be greater and God's glory more visible.

God is very jealous of the praises of his saints. As he bathes himself in their tears, so he delights himself in their joys. He loves to hear their praises as well as their prayers.

And you know the greater the straits out of which God helps and delivers, the more the hearts of the saints are enlarged with praises to him.

God does wonders for his church when he can do the church the most good and work the most complete deliverance for them. This is the time for God to do wonders for his church.

You see this in the narrative of Pharaoh. God could have brought about a deliverance for Israel by disabling his chariots as soon as Pharaoh led his army out of Egypt. But had he done so, this would not have been such a complete deliverance as they afterward experienced. This way God would have delivered them from that present trouble, but their enemies would have still been alive, and they would have heard of them again. But God instead allowed them to pursue the Israelites by following them unto the Red Sea so that he might work a complete and absolute deliverance for them. This was a great demonstration of the wonders of God.

Observe in Micah 4:11-13 that God allows nations, many nations to gather themselves together against Zion. Why? Certainly, his enemies thought they would defile Zion. But they did not know the thoughts of the Lord, they did not understand the counsel of God. For God allows them to gather themselves together for this end, for the complete ruination of his enemies and the complete deliverance of his church. They do not know the thoughts and plans of the Lord. They gathered themselves together; and yet the text says that God gathers them. They gathered themselves to ruin the church, but God gathers them to ruin themselves.

A fourth time when God does wonderful things for his church is when the enemies of the church are the most enraged, expecting the most success against the church and people of God.

You see this in the verses before the text (verses 9, 10), "when the enemy said in his heart, I will pursue, I will overtake, I will divide the spoil, my lust shall be satisfied on them; I will draw my sword, my hand shall destroy them." They expressed their fury and rage and promised themselves good success in it all.

So the time was here ripe for God to do wonders, which you see in the next verse, "Thou didst blow with thy wind, the sea covered them, they sank as lead in the mighty waters." Such was their rage, their fury. And yet now was the time for God to show a wondrous deliverance of his church: a wonder of wisdom in the discovery of their evil plot and a wonder of mercy in the disposing of it.

When God's people are brought low, when all human help fails, when the arm of flesh is weak, when the stream of second causes runs dry ... then it is God's time to show a wonder for their relief. When we cannot be relieved without a wonder, then God works wonders for our relief. You see this in Deuteronomy 32:35-36, "The Lord shall judge his people, and repent himself concerning his servants: when he sees that their power is gone, and there is none shut up nor left." When Israel was brought to those straits, the Red Sea before them, the Egyptians behind them, and mountains on each side of them, Moses said, "Fear not, stand still, and see the salvation of the Lord," (Exod. 14:13). It is as if he had said, "You are now in straits such that your extremities are great. So now is the time for God to help. Now is God's time to do wonders for you."

We might refer to two times, or timing from two perspectives: 1) man's time, and 2) God's time. Man's time is whenever we are in need, whenever we are in trouble. But God's time is only when all helps fail; when no relief is in the arm of the flesh, then all is in God.

God stands ever ready to put forth himself in desperate cases, because then his mercy and power will be most conspicuous, his people most thankful, and deliverance most glorious.

It is an old, experienced truth, *man's extremity is God's opportunity.* The depth of man's misery calls for the depth of God's mercy.

It may be observed in all ecclesiastical histories, that when deliverance approached, persecution was the most intense. The scribes and pharisees blasphemed the most when their kingdom was nearest ruin. It is like the devil who roars most when his time is shortest. The greatest darkness is before the morning watch. When the morning is darkest, then comes the day; when trouble is greatest, then comes deliverance.

In the case of the Israelites, when their task of making bricks from clay was doubled, then was Moses sent to deliver them.

God's promises are never nearer fulfilling than when to sense and reason they seem furthest from fulfilling. This was Abraham's case, when at God's command he was about to sacrifice his son Isaac.

Another time when God does wonders for his church, is when God's people rise up together in a mighty spirit of prayer to seek him.

You see this in the deliverance of the church out of the Babylonian captivity. In this deliverance God expressed many wonders of mercy to his church. At this time, God also raised up a mighty spirit of prayer in them to seek deliverance. (Dan. 9:2-3, Psalm 102:13-17). "Thou shalt arise and have mercy upon Zion: for the time to favor her, the set time is come." Why? How can we know that now is the time? He shows us in the 14th verse. "For thy servants take pleasure in the stones, and favor the dust thereof." That is, they mourn, and they pray. And therefore, it is time for his help and deliverance, as you see in the 17th verse, "Thou shalt regard the prayer of the desolate, and not despise their prayer." So, when God stirs up the hearts of his people to seek him, it is an evident demonstration that he will do great things for that people. He has told us that he will not forsake those who seek him; when the eyes and hearts of God's people are enlarged with sorrow, then is God's mercy enlarged with deliverance, ready to deliver.

Wicked men have a measure of sin to fill, as God said of the Amorites, "The iniquity of the Amorites is not yet full." And Christ to the scribes and pharisees, "Fill you up the measure of your fathers," (Matt. 23:22). When the harvest is ripe; then will God put in his sickle, as in Joel 3:13, "Put in the sickle, for the harvest is ripe; for the wickedness is great." God has a bag for the sins of the wicked (Job 14:17). And he has a bottle for the tears of his servants (Ps. 56:8). He bags up sins, and he bottles up tears. And when his bag is full of the transgressions of the wicked, and his bottle is full of the tears of the saints, then salvation will come to Zion; then will God move to relieve and succor his church.

When wicked men are ripe for destruction and the church ripe for deliverance, then God will perform his whole work upon Zion and will punish the fruit of the proud doer.

When the glory of God is mightily concerned, he works wonders to further his worship, his truth, his cause. Though God will not do it for us per se, yet he will do it for his own name's sake. He will not allow his glory to be compromised.

And this was the argument Joshua had in Joshua 7:8-9. When Israel sinned, and God delivered them up to their enemies, he pleads with God, "Lord, what will become of thy great name! Though Israel deserves not that thou shouldest stand out for them; yet let not thy glory suffer for their sin; but let thy name, which is so much concerned, draw you out to relieve and help."

As the prophet says in Isaiah 48:9-11, "For my name's sake I will defer my anger; and for my praise will I refrain for thee, that I do not cut you off. For my own sake, even for my own sake will I do it: for how should my name be polluted? I will not give my glory to another." And 2 Kings 18:35, "Who are there among the gods of the countries that have delivered their country out of my hand, that the Lord should deliver Jerusalem out of my hand?" Here you see when it was God's glory that was of concern, to preserve his glory he shows a wonder to help them.

And happy are they, whose deliverance is joined with God's glory. Though God will not always deliver for our sake, yet he will deliver for his glory, for his own name's sake (Ezek. 36:32).

Part 7: Will God Do a Wonder for Us?

How can we know whether God will work a wonder for us? I will first give you the grounds of my fears and then the grounds of my hopes, that God will not desert us at this time.

The grounds of fear are either spiritual or natural.

In terms of spiritual, they include the universality of sin, the arrogance of sin, and the obstinance of sin among us.

Regarding the universality of sins, all people, all places are filled with all kinds of sins. The land is full of adulteries, oppression, injustice, pride, profaning the sabbath, and contempt of God's ordinances. The world is full of drunkenness; the whole land is defiled with blood: prince and people, magistrates and ministers, great and small, rich and poor; we are all defiled with sin. We may take up the complaint of the prophet in Isaiah 1:6, "From the sole of the foot, even to the head, there is no soundness in it, but wounds and bruises, and putrefying sores: they have not been closed, nor bound up, nor mollified with ointment."

But there are four sins especially that threaten evil to us, and those more immediately concern God and his worship: idolatry, profaning his ordinances, profaning his sabbath, and contempt and abuse of his ministers. Any of these would be enough to sink a nation, even if they were guilty of nothing more. But then you add to that the arrogance of sin, when men are not ashamed to swear, to drink, to prophane the sabbath, to treat his ordinances with contempt. In fact, many are more ashamed to pray than others are to swear.

Thirdly, add to all this the obstinance of sin. For sin is not only universal and arrogant, but it has grown obstinate, stubborn, and incorrigible. Insomuch that neither mercy nor judgment, word nor works, promises nor threats will be powerful enough to persuade men. Sin may be said to be incorrigible when it has grown too strong for those means God has set up to keep it down. When sin is too strong for the ordinances and offices God has set up for the suppressing and keeping down of sin, then it is incorrigible (Jer. 6).

It is now as it was when the Lord complained of Ephraim in Hosea 7:1, "When I would have healed Israel, then the iniquity of Ephraim was discovered."

The schisms and divisions among us weaken us further. If we had joined our mutual strength against our common adversaries and not turned the heat of contention upon ourselves, we would not now have been so weak, nor our adversaries so strong.

But I hope we will be like sheep, that though a fair day has scattered us all over the field one from another, yet a storm will drive us together again.

Then there is the willful blindness among men who will not see how much their religion, their liberties, and privileges are at risk. Or if they do, they do not seem to care enough to risk everything to secure and uphold them.

Add to all this, all the missed opportunities. As Christ said, "O Jerusalem! Jerusalem! Had you known, even you, at least in this your day, the things that belong to your peace! But now they are hid from your eyes," (Luke 19:41-42). There are some special times when God puts advantages before his people. And if those opportunities are lost, they may never again be recovered.

These are the chief grounds of my fear that give way to suspicion that God will not do wonders for us.

And yet to these let me add the grounds of my *hope*. The arguments that may persuade us, and the reasons that may induce us to believe that God will do wonders, are these five.

First, the origin of wonders is our God. As they come from God, they exude the goodness of his nature. He is gracious and merciful – gracious in himself, and exceedingly gracious to his saints.

Though we are not promised a particular deliverance at this time, yet we may throw ourselves on the good nature of God, that he will not deliver us up into the hands of cruel, merciless, and bloody men who seek our ruin.

Though our sins are many, and God might discipline us as we deserve, yet he loves his people so much as not to put us into the hands of such cruel men to be punished.

You have some ground for this suggestion in Deut. 32:27. When God was highly displeased with Israel and threatened to destroy them, he was concerned that their enemies would deal too harshly with them and that they would destroy them rather than just punish them. Though Israel had sinned, God did not want to make use of sinners to punish their sin, for he knew the mercies of the wicked were cruel mercies.

A second argument from God concerns God's glory. It is not only our good, but *his own glory*, that is concerned. So, though he may not do it for us, yet he will do it for his own name's sake.

There are many things he will not do for our sakes but yet he will for his own sake. You see this in Ezek. 36:32, "Not for your sakes do I do this, O house of Israel." But though he would not do it for their sakes, yet he would do it because his glory was concerned; he would do it for his own name's sake. We find similar expressions in Exod. 32:12, Deut. 9:28, and Isa. 48:9-11. Though Israel had provoked God, yet for his own glory he would deliver them. God's glory in his truth, in his worship, in his saints, in his ordinances. They are all concerned at this time.

There are arguments taken from the church of God in general. And that is that the good of most of the Reformed churches in the Christian world depend on the welfare of England. And in a great measure, upon the good success of this present parliament. And therefore, seeing that the preservation and deliverance of England is of such public concern, it may persuade us that God would rather perform a wonder, than not preserve England. We never read that God destroyed any nation that was in the process of reforming and turning back to him. And it has pleased God at this time to set us up a choice assembly chosen by prayer, brought together by prayer, and held together and preserved to this day by the power of prayer.

A third argument is from ourselves. You know what our condition had been before; the remembrance of it is fresh. God heard the cry of our souls, pitied us in our low estate, and showed mercy to us. And so, reason says that if God planned to destroy us, he would never have done this much for us.

That which God has done is an earnest to us, and an engagement upon God to go on to finish what he has begun to do for us already.

Shall we think he has brought us out of Egypt to destroy us in the wilderness? Shall we think the sun of mercy has shined on us only to warm our heads against a storm? Shall we think he has exalted us that he might lay us low in the end?

Indeed, God has done so with the wicked. But we never read that he has so done with his own people.

Shall we think he has delivered us from lesser to reserve us to greater judgments? Has he freed us from rods just to whip us with scorpions? Delivered us from lesser evils to ruin us at once?

God may do this with wicked men, but I do not think he would ever do this with his own.

A fourth argument taken from our experience to encourage us to hope that God will do a wonder for us is that there is a stock of prayers going out and laid up for the good of this church and nation.

Many prayers have been made. And if the prayer of one Moses could do so much, what will the prayers of so many thousands accomplish?

A fifth argument is that from time-to-time God draws out the graces of his people. And do you think that God will draw out the graces of his people for their destruction? We read God hardens wicked men to destruction, but never that he makes the heart tender for the purposes of their ruin. Men have perished because of their fear, deserting the cause of God. But none have gone down to destruction who put their trust in God and courageously stood by it.

Did Esther lose anything by her obedience? Did Daniel? Did the three children? It brought them into the fire but also preserved them in the fire. Nothing was consumed but their bands; not even one hair was singed.

The fourth category of arguments that supports whether God will do a wonder for us is taken from our enemies.

When Satan's rage is at its most violent, it is a sign that his time on this earth to deceive men is growing short. As Rev. 12:12 states, "Woe to the inhabitants of the earth," (that is, to the wicked and the ungodly). "But rejoice ye heavens," (that is, the saints and people of God). Why? "For the devil is come down, having great wrath." But how can this be a matter of rejoicing? Because it means his time is short. So, when men grow more evil in their malice and blasphemies, they become an abomination to men. And God himself will soon unburden the nation of them.

You may say this is not enough to persuade us that God will do a wonder for us, for we sometimes read that God gave over the godly into the hands of wicked men to be punished. Yes, God sometimes gives up a people to others, who have been greater sinners than themselves. He sometimes gives up one wicked nation to another that was even more wicked. But God typically does this after his people have been exceedingly disobedient, and after he sends his prophets to warn them, to humble and reform them.

Part 8: Wonders at the Latter End of the World

The fifth argument to induce us to hope that God will now do a wonder for us is taken from the consideration of those great things which God has promised to do for his church and people in this latter end of the world.

Indeed, God has done much for his people in all ages of the world; you can see those wonders that have been recorded. But all these are nothing in comparison to those which he has engaged himself to do for his people in the hereafter.

The world is the stage on which God will act out all his wonders; and it cannot be long before this frame of time is dissolved, and this stage taken down. If the Apostle John lived in the last hour, surely ours is the final minutes.

Yet God will not take down the stage until all has transpired which he has promised his church. And again, I will say that God has engaged himself to destroy that man of sin in order to make his church glorious.

Take it upon yourself to read how much God has promised to do for his church in Isaiah 60. Until now the church has been buried under reproach, scorn, and persecution. Up to this point, the church of God has been subjected to sufferings, prisons, and martyrdom. To date, the church of God has been like Noah's ark, tossed along on the devouring waves of troubles and persecutions. And the saints under the altar (the blood of the slain) cry, "how long Lord, holy and true!" Though they suffer, they give God the glory for his truth and faithfulness. Though he may defer the accomplishment of what he has promised, yet his promises are true.

Has God engaged himself to make his churches glorious before the end of all things? And is this day so near the end? Notwithstanding the present oppositions and troubles, God is now coming with mercy and deliverance to his church and his people. For he has not left us without hope that the work has begun — that mighty spirit of prayer which God pours out on his people, that increase of light and knowledge, the increase of converts within these few years, are all signs of the rising condition of the church. As in Acts 7:17, the Israelites grew and multiplied in Egypt when the time of their deliverance drew near. Their growing was a sign of their rising; their increase confirmed that the promised mercy was not far off.

And these are hopeful signs, that the day of the church's redemption draws near. As Christ said of the fig tree, when you see the fig tree bud and put forth her leaves, know that summer is near. And when you see these things in the church, you may know that the church's redemption is at hand. God will not rest until he has made his church glorious in the earth.

And now having told you my thoughts, and that which persuades with me to hope that God will do a wonder for us, I must remind you again that we may suffer many pains and much opposition, and perhaps even some blood, before these things. God will save us from trouble by trouble. He will bring us through a sea, and through the wilderness unto Canaan. Yet I will say as Joshua did in Numbers 14:8, "If the Lord has any delight in us, he will bring us into this land."

God *seldom* does great things without great commotions. When Paul and Silas were delivered from prison, it was accompanied by an earthquake. And we must not forsake a good cause because of opposition. We must not jump ship because the winds blow.

Assure yourselves of this: though earth and hell should fight against you, your safety lies in God's hands and in God's cause; and there is no safety elsewhere.

These things I suggest to you, by way of caution so that when you see these things, you may not be troubled. As Christ said to his disciples, "these things I tell you before that when they do come to pass, your hearts may not be troubled," so these things I tell you before as well. So that when you see storms come, oppositions and troubles arise, remain steadfast in your faith in God's goodness and glory. This is necessary advice, lest oppositions and seeming contradictions of God's proceedings should weaken your faith and move you from your own steadfastness. We are too apt to live by sense and not by faith; by works and not by the word; by God's outward appearances and proceedings of providence and not by promises. And therefore, our faith wanes or increases according to what God allows in the ways of his providence like what you see with Joseph and with Israel in Egypt, where the promise spoke one thing and God's outward proceedings seemed to speak another. When we react emotionally in cycles like this, we give up all hope and remembrance of God's promises given in his word, like David did when he believed that he would indeed perish by the hand of Saul.

This is why we need to learn this lesson: to shut our eyes to the works of God and instead look upon *the word of God:* not only to look upon the outward proceedings of providence, but upon the stability and truth of the *promise* and conclude, because *it is* promised, so shall it be even if all secondary means through which the promise may be performed say it shall not be.

God promised that antichrist shall be defeated. He promised to make his church glorious. And though circumstances may seem to say otherwise, we should not let this weaken our faith in believing the truth of what God has promised.

If you put a straight stick into the water, it appears to be crooked. But reason tells you that it is straight, for that is how it was when you first put it in. Likewise, when outward circumstances seem to say that God is against us, why should we not by faith conclude that he is for us based on his word?

The outward face of things may cause the church to fear. But God has a purpose to do great things for his church. As we read in Joel 2:21, "Fear not, O land; be glad, and rejoice; for the Lord will do great things for you." It was a time of joy regarding God's purpose, and yet a time of fear in respect to their present apprehensions. God had a purpose to do great things for them, and yet the face and outward appearance of things possessed the church with fear.

You see what Christ said in Luke 21:25, "There shall be signs in the sun, in the moon, in the stars; and upon the earth distress of nations; the sea and waters roaring, men's hearts failing them for fear, and for looking after the things that shall come upon the earth, for the powers of heaven shall be shaken." And yet Christ also reminded us that when these things begin to come to pass, we are to look up and lift our heads, for our redemption is near.

Here Christ turns the saddest and most difficult perplexities that ever the world shall see into a doctrine of *comfort* to his church, because all these things are preparatory to the redemption of the church.

This is the admonition I give you, that whatever oppositions, whatever troubles, whatever evils we meet with in the way of deliverance we should not allow them to trouble us. We should not allow our hearts to be discouraged, for this is the way in which God will do you good. He makes all your evil and trouble subservient to good.

What the apostle said of his bonds in Philippians 1:12 I may say of all oppositions, "The things which have happened to me, have fallen out to the furtherance of the gospel." His prison was the gospel's liberty, his difficulties and chains the gospel's enlargement, and his abasements, the gospel's advancements.

As we say, the choicest blessings come out of the fire of afflictions. And so, the greatest deliverances come out of the greatest oppositions.

Part 9: Application of the Doctrine

We now come to the application of this doctrine. It informs us of the greatness of our God in terms of his power, wisdom, mercy, and faithfulness toward his people. All these attributes are visibly declared in every wonder God does for his church. God demonstrates the greatness of his power in every wonder he does for them. If a man were able to do it, it would be no wonder.

God demonstrates the greatness of his wisdom in every wonder as well. His wisdom is evident in the manner the wonder is conceived as well as in the timing of it, as when the situations are desperate, or in such times when he gets himself the most glory and does us the most good.

Finally, his wisdom is demonstrated in terms of how he delivers these wonders, means we would have never thought of or, if we had, would have seemed to us too insignificant to yield such a great deliverance.

God also demonstrates an abundance of free mercy as noted in Psalm 136 (a psalm of praises for wonders). And at the end of every wonder noted, the refrain echoes, "for his mercy endures forever."

God demonstrates his truth and faithfulness to his church. And all the deliverances of God are performances of promises. Further, these instances and experiences prove the truth of the promise and show the faithfulness of the promiser to us. They are witnesses to both. "By the mouth of two or three witnesses every word shall be established," said the apostle. God is truth personified; you may believe him without a witness. But even then, he has not left himself without witness; nor has God left any word without witness.

There is never a truth, never a promise in the word that has not been made good by a thousand experiences. We have a book of experiences to annex to the book of promises, of the many wonders which God has in all ages performed for his people, all of which demonstrates both the faithfulness and the truth of God and his promises to us.

Further, these truths inform us of the blessed and happy condition of the saints who have interest in a God who can do wonders for them. Though your troubles are too big for man, they are not for God. Your miseries may be above the supply of creatures, but they cannot be above the power of God. He can do wonders; he can do that which man cannot do.

Though you have no ordinary means of help, yet you have interest in a God who can do extraordinary things; he can do extraordinary things in an ordinary way and by ordinary means. I may say with the psalmist, "Blessed are the people whose God is the Lord," (Ps. 144:15).

These truths inform us of how precious the saints are to God and what love he bears to his church that he will do wonders for them. He does wonders for their preservation from trouble and wonders for their deliverance out of trouble.

The common blessings of life are not sufficient to show God's love. He causes his sun to shine and his rain to fall on the good as well as the evil. But when God exercises the greatness of his power, wisdom, truth, and mercy in the wonders he does for his church, this is evidence of the degree of love he has for them.

Wicked men may be subjects on whom he exercises the wonders of his justice and power, as it was with Pharaoh. But the saints are those for whom he exercises the wonders of his mercy. God's wonders are for the good, or for them in a good way.

This also tells us that the conditions of God's people can never be so sad and uncomfortable as to despair of help and relief, since we have a God who does wonders for us. Our condition is never so low that a wonder may raise us up again.

We may be hopeless and helpless in terms of creature supplies and reliefs. But we can never be hopeless nor helpless in terms of God. For when creature-helps fail, God turns us from sense to faith, from reasoning to believing, from creatures to himself. He tells us not to look at things below, but on things above. Even David encouraged himself in the Lord his God, for he knew that in the most hopeless condition, there is deliverance with the Lord.

O that we could learn, at such a time as this, to live by faith and not by sense, to shut our eyes to physical evidence and look upon the word of God. We should be strong in God and find encouragement from him when we see nothing but discouragements around us.

We are too apt to live by our senses and not by faith. So, depending on whether God shows or restrains himself and his wonders in the ways of his providence, our faith either wanes or increases.

We are like Hagar in that when the bottle is dry, we sit down and cry. Whereas, on the contrary; we should trust in God.

1. In the weakness of means. Because though there is an abundance of weakness here on earth, there is strength in God. Weakness and strength are all one with God.

2. In the lack of means. Though means may be lacking, God can create means. He can even do his work without means if he chooses.

3. In the opposition of means. When the promise says, "it shall be," though all secondary means whereby this promise could be affected says it shall not be, yet we are to rest upon God and his promise.

God often speaks one thing to sense and another to faith. He is never in appearance what he is in truth. A perfect example is the children of Israel at the Red Sea. With everything they could see within the realm of sense and reason, the situation was hopeless. They would die. And yet Moses said, "Fear not. Stand still and see the salvation of the Lord." It may appear from circumstances that God means to bring hurt to his people, yet in time it is evident that his purposes are only to do his children good.

As the prophet states in Jer. 29:11, "I know the thoughts I have thought toward you, saith the Lord, thoughts of peace and not of trouble: even to give you a desired end." In other words, though my providences may seem to be evil, yet my thoughts are good; though my ways are not your ways, yet my purposes are peace, to give you at the last an expected end.

These truths inform us that there is no ground for wicked men to glory in any supposed advantages which they think they may have against the church and people of God, for God can work wonders for his church and people.

This was the case with the Egyptians who had many advantages against the people of God. Further, they promised themselves certain and infallible success. They said they would pursue, they would overtake, and they would divide the spoil. But God demonstrated his power through a wonder, destroying all their pride and all their hopes in the dust. What began in pride ended in shame.

This truth also makes us aware of the duty to obedience that lies with those people for whom God shall do wonders.

First of all, we should *love* him. God expressed his love toward us while we were still in our sin, so as his children we are beholden to love him in return.

Further, we should *engage* in thankfulness. As Psalm 111:4 states, "He has done his wonderful works to be remembered." As if he had said, "This is the end, I did these wondrous works so that you should remember them. If you would not have remembered them, I would not have done them." As in the speech of Seneca, "the giver may soon forget he gave but the receiver must never forget that he has received."

God has done many wonders for his people where he expressed his wisdom, power, mercy, and justice. And yet he continues as freely in mercy as if every mercy were the first mercy he had bestowed. But do we forget what we have received? If so, God will remember that he has given; God remembers what he has given when his people forget they have received.

If you do not want God to remember what he has given against you, then remember what you have received from him. This will *remind* you to be thankful.

Since God does wonders for his church, we are moved to *trust* him, to pray to him, to hope in him, and to wait upon him.

Psalm 78 and Nehemiah 9 both chronicle the great wonders which God has done for his church and his people. These remembrances of what God has already done for his people is a great and mighty encouragement.

As the judgments of God upon the wicked are recorded to deter us from sin, so the mercies and deliverances of the church are recorded to encourage us to believe and trust him in like difficulties.

Can our condition be more difficult than Israel's was at the Red Sea? Than David's? Than Jehoshaphat's? Than the churches in Haman's time? And yet God delivered them that we might be encouraged to trust him in like straits and difficulties.

And as we have encouragement from the experience of God's wonderful deliverance of others, so we have encouragement from the wonderful deliverance of ourselves.

It is true that we ought to trust God though we have never tried him, though we have never experience wonders from him. But when he helps our faith by former experiences, this should strengthen our confidence and make us to go to God as a tried friend.

Were we but well-read in the story of our lives, we might have a bible of our own drawn out of the experiences of God's dealings with us personally. We would be able to say in any difficulty and distress, "I will trust God in this difficulty. I will trust in him in this present distress. I have tried him and have found him true; he never failed me. And because he has been my help, under the shadow of his wings will I rejoice."

A second encouragement is from the power of God. He can do wonders. He not only has, but he does wonders still. "The arm of the Lord is not shortened that he cannot save. What he has done, he can do. He is still as wise, as powerful, as faithful, as merciful as ever he was. There is no shadow of change in him. There is nothing above his skill nor his power.

It is our sin alone that hinders the current of mercy, that stops the stream of God's mercy: our unbelief, our neglect of duty, our unthankfulness, our pride, *etc.* When we remove these, mercy comes again. You have a renewed place for it. As you see in Judges 10:10-16, God had often delivered them. He had done many wonders for them, as he tells them here. And they were now again in a new distress, and therefore cry out to God. But God tells them they had walked unworthy of former deliverances, and therefore he would deliver them no more. After hearing this, they once again confess their sins before God. They humble themselves and reform their evil ways. And then, as the text states, God delivers them yet again.

This may well mirror our own condition in that God has brought about many deliverances for us. And yet when we find ourselves faced with new difficulties, our sins may stand as an obstacle that hinders God's mercies. But if we humble ourselves and turn from our wicked ways, God will be grieved for our misery as he was for theirs.

A third encouragement that we have available to us to trust in is God's love to his church and his many precious promises to them. His church is dear to him; we are his spouse, his members, those he died for by choice, by purchase, by gift, and by covenant.

And being his, he will do great things for us also. God's love for his church is the only ground of our faith and hope to expect mercies from him.

These truths also assure us that the reason God allows wicked men to plan evil schemes against the church, and even to carry out those schemes, is that they are already set for execution. God doesn't choose to disrupt their plans because he can do wonders. He may allow them to go on, but they will never get the advantage over God.

When men see an adversary they can easily master when they please, they will let them go on, taking no notice of them. For they know the further they let them go, the fuller and more complete their overthrow will be at the end.

In a similar way, God allows wicked men to go on because he knows he can overtake them before they reach their goal. So he can let them go on; he can let them bring their designs to fruition because they can never become too great for his power to conquer them. He can dash their plans in their strength as well as in their weakness. This too is a wonder of God.

This is why God allowed Pharaoh to proceed with his plans to overtake the Israelites at the Red Sea. He did not stop him in his preparations, nor hinder him in his proceedings, but let him fully fulfill his plan. For God knew he would have him at the last; he would show a wonder and destroy him and all his army in the sea.

It was also so with Haman. God could have thwarted his counsel in the beginning; he could have set the king against it. But he lets him go on and bring his design to fruition and then declares a wonder, ruining him and his counsel too.

This is the reason God allows wicked men to go on, gather themselves together, bring their designs to the utmost because he can break them in the end as well as in the beginning.

God's people are dear to him. They are his inheritance, his portion, his jewels, his treasure that were bought with no less than the price of his own blood. As the apostle said, "you were not redeemed with silver and gold, but with the precious blood of Christ," (1 Peter 1:19). Do you then think that God will not preserve his people? Yes, he certainly will, and will do wonders to preserve them. Assure yourselves, God will never desert his cause, his church, his people. When wicked men seek to destroy the people of God, then God will fight for his own against those who are enemies of the church of God.

God promised that he will never leave us nor forsake us. He said he will be with us as he was with Joseph in prison. And not as one to just observe or take notice only, but as one to relieve and help us. His power shall be with us, his wisdom, *etc.*

And as he is with his church, so he is against the enemies of it. His power is against them, before whom all the nations of the earth are but as the drop of a bucket. And woe be to them whom God is against.

He has a rod of iron, a scepter of power, an arm of strength to crush all his adversaries in pieces. Like Pilate's wife said to her husband, "have nothing to do with that just man," so I say to you, have nothing to do, by way of offence, against the church and the people of God. You will do nothing but cause your own ruin. God said of his church, that whoever raised their hand against it shall be crushed to pieces. Though all the nations of the world be gathered together against her, yet all will be to no purpose. Their very attempt shall be their destruction. Just like it was with pharaoh who followed the children of Israel so long, that there was no return at the last; he was buried in the waters.

All the encounters of wicked men against the church are nothing but a piece of straw set ablaze with a torch of fire that burns themselves up. There was never a man who struck against the church who was not struck down by its own recoil. They dig graves to bury themselves in, make rods for their own backs, and pave a way for their own destruction. As in Isaiah 54:15-17, "Behold, the enemy shall gather himself, but without me: whosoever shall gather himself against you shall fall. No weapon made against you shall prosper; every tongue that shall rise against you in judgement, you shall condemn. This is the heritage of the Lord's servants."

Know that God will work wonders for the deliverance of his church and for the destruction of the wicked. So let this encourage you in these times of danger and trouble. There is no cause for fear, seeing we have God on our side who can do wonders for us. As David says in Psalm 20:7, "Some trust in chariots and some in horses, but we will remember the name of the Lord our God."

Knowing this, what are castles and forts? What are multitudes of men? What are riches? All this, and whatever else an adversary may have to glory in, is but fleshly strength. But you have a God who can do wonders for you. Therefore, "I will boast in God," (the prophet says) "all day long."

Do not give way to doubt. You do not have cause to fear if you look above, as well as below. If you converse with heaven as well as with earth. Therefore, fear is unbefitting a Christian, one who truly believes in God, you who have so great a God that can do wonders for you. Further, a good cause should be matched with a good courage. As Luther said, "if our cause be not good, let us desist, and leave it. If it be good, let us go on courageously." The cause of Christ and a coward's heart do not belong together. God's people are too apt to this. Therefore, Christ steels the heart of his disciples against it., "Fear not little flock." Though a little flock, yet there is no cause to fear since we have such a strong shepherd. Isaiah 41:13-14 says, "For I the Lord thy God will hold thy right hand, saying unto thee, Fear not; I will help thee.

Though our enemies be full of rage and violence, and though they seek our ruin, God can calm them and still them as he did the sea, and as he did Esau when he came against Jacob. God can also stop them in their way. "He that sets bounds to the sea and says, 'here is where you shall come and no further, and here shall you stop your proud waves,'" can stop them in their tracks.

He can turn them and change their hearts, as he did Paul's when he went out breathing threatenings and slaughter against the church of Christ (Acts 9).

He can overturn them and overpower them. Even when they fight with expertise, he will be above them (Exod. 18:11).

As there is no cause to fear, so there is much less any cause of discouragement, for in these days of evil God can do wonders.

You will never know what God can do, nor what he will do, until you stand in need. God loves to appear in time of extremity; he loves to put forth himself in desperate cases.

As the shipman's star never appears but before death, so God's power never reveals itself until a dissolution and death of secondary means.

When we have the sentence of death passed upon us in terms of helps and means, then it is God's time to step in, to recover and relieve us.

The Apostle Paul indicates this very truth in 2 Cor. 1:9, "We received the sentence of death in ourselves, that we might not trust in ourselves, but in God who raises the dead." We would not know what God can do without the knowledge of what man cannot do. We cannot know the power of God without experiencing the weakness of man. And without the greatness of our misery, we could not have experiences of God's mercy. How many would say, I would not lose the experiences of God's goodness due to the sad condition I was in for a thousand worlds? I would rather go through a thousand such sad circumstances than not know even one of those experiences of his mercy in it. At these times you shall have experience of God's power, wisdom, mercy, faithfulness, all which are drawn out to help in need.

If you study God's word, you will find that often God's people have failed in the strength of means, but never read that they failed in weakness. And the reason is because they trusted God in the one and were self-confident in the other.

It is our nature that when means are weak and wanting, we run to God for help. But when means are strong to bring purposes to pass, we are apt to rest upon them.

This was so with King Asa (2 Chron. 14-16). When he was weak, he trusted in God. When he felt confident, he trusted in his own strength. Weak means were successful because his faith brought God into them, and his strong means were unfruitful because he made a god of them, trusting in them instead of the true God. Not to trust in God in the strength of means is to neglect God. Not to trust in him during weakness of means is to limit God.

God loves to appear when none else will and when none else can. This was David's argument in Psalm 22:11, "Be not far from me, for trouble is near; for there is none to help." As it was said of the redemption of the church from sin, so it may be said of her deliverance from trouble, "when he looks about, and sees no man, then his right hand shall bring salvation." He will do a wonder to save you. Though there be mountains of opposition in the way, God handles these mountains in four ways:

1. He melts the mountains; he dissolves them as water (Isa. 64:3).

2. He lays them into plains. That is, he makes those mountains which were before impassable to be no opposition at all (Zech. 4:7).

3. He destroys the mountains and all those who stand to oppose God's church and people (Isa. 41:14-15).

4. He passes right over them. He steps over the head of all those who stand in the way to the deliverance of his church (Song of Songs 2:8).

Therefore, do not worry over the greatness of the opposition. Though there are many mountains of opposition, God can melt them, or he can level them, or destroy them, or skip over them. And one way or another God will do so, for the deliverance of his church.

Part 10: Three Final Lessons

Since God does wonders for his people, such as no one else can, let us learn these three lessons: thankfulness, obedience, and dependence.

1. Here is the lesson of thankfulness to be learned. We stand before God this day, having received an abundance of his mercies. Many mercies God has bestowed on us and long continues to us. Many evils he kept from us, and many evils he has freed us from. We stand before God this day because of the many glorious deliverances he has wrought for us.

God has revealed the wonders of his wisdom, the wonders of his power, the wonders of his mercy and love in many a glorious deliverance. And now, our souls being warmed with the sense and consideration of these wonders, should burst forth into a flame of praises to our God!

But it is often with us as it was with the children of Israel. We often seek his help but forget him when times are good. So that which should be a means of drawing us nearer to him is instead a means of further distancing us from him. Considering his demonstrations of mercy, an unthankful heart is a great sin, one which would justly stop his flow of mercy.

Ingratitude is against the very principles of humanity and is the abuse of a good God. That which gives birth to mercy is prayer, and that which gives breath to mercy is thankfulness. Mercy is short lived when men are unthankful.

The second lesson we should learn in light of his mercy is obedience. Let the mercy of God quicken you to duty. Look upon every mercy as a further engagement to you to walk more holy and closer to God.

As all the spiritual mercies of God in election, redemption, justification, sanctification, and promises of glorification, were all given as engagements to obedience, so it is with all the temporal mercies. As 1 Samuel 12:24 says, "Therefore fear the Lord, and serve him in truth with all your hearts, and consider what great things he has done for you." When mercies spur us on to duty, God is pleased to shower us with mercy.

Let these mercies also teach us to depend upon God. A lack of trusting our good God was what he blamed the children of Israel for. Notwithstanding the great and wonderful works he had done in their sight, they did not trust him. Everything he did for them collectively was not enough to work up their hearts to believe in his goodness and trust in him.

David blames them for the same in Psalm 78:19- 20, "They spoke against God; can God furnish a table in the wilderness? Indeed, he smote the rock, that the waters gushed out and the streams overflowed: but can he give bread also? Can he provide flesh for his people?" One would think this a senseless reasoning. But unbelief is a senseless sin. Was not the wonders God had already demonstrated to them not sufficient for what followed?

The same power was required for the doing of the one as for the other; and when they had seen the power of God work the greater, isn't it strange that they would doubt he could do the lesser? But herein lies the baseness of our spirit; though God has given us ever so many experiences, yet we are still to seek dependence on him. And without further grace we cannot do it.

We think, when we are in straits and difficulties, if God would but help us through this strait, if he would but relieve us in this difficulty, we should never distrust him again while we live. We would depend on him even in the saddest of conditions. But these are present thoughts. And without future assistances and supplies, we are as likely to doubt his help in future difficulties as we were in the first.

God has demonstrated many great things for us: every one of them should be a life-mercy, a standing-mercy, a mercy to be set up to encourage us to depend on him forever. We should be able to draw on these mercies in every strait, to feed upon them in every future difficulty.

God demonstrated his power and goodness to his people by rescuing them from pharaoh and his army at the Red Sea before they entered the wilderness. He did this to strengthen their faith and dependence on him for the many additional difficulties they would be facing in the wilderness.

That mercy is never well digested that is not fed upon. Without feeding on God's wondrous mercies to us, we miss the spiritual nourishment to be derived from it. So, when you find yourself facing new difficulties, return to the former mercies and experiences to feed upon to refresh your faith and to enable you to depend upon God afresh.

He that is not a good treasurer of mercies has nothing to draw upon in future difficulties. But he who lays up experiences and makes use of them to feed upon and draw strength from is enabled to depend on God in all future difficulties.

You see this demonstrated with David when he chose to fight Goliath, "God delivered me out of the paw of the lion, and out of the paw of the bear: and he will deliver me out of the hand of this Philistine." And "because he has been my helper, therefore under the shadow of his wings will I rejoice."

In terms of passing this duty of dependence upon you, there are two snares which you should be aware of: beware of obliterating the notions of God, and beware of burying the remembrance of his works.

Had Moses seen God and had the same notions and apprehensions of God at the rock that he had at the Red Sea (which was a far greater difficulty than fetching water out of the rock), he could have trusted in God for that, as well as for the former. But his thoughts and conceptions of God were, for the present, darkened and therefore he did not draw on that former mercy to trust God for water out of the rock.

Likewise, if David had had the same trust in God when he pretended to be mad for fear of Abimelech, the king of Gath, or when he was pursued by Saul and wrote these words, "I shall one day perish by the hand of Saul," as he had when he said in Psalm 27:1-3, "The lord is my light, and my salvation, whom shall I fear? The lord is the strength of my life: of whom shall I be afraid? When the wicked who are mine enemies, and my foes came upon me, to eat up my flesh, they stumbled and fell. Though a host pitched against me, my heart should not be afraid: though war be raised against me, in this will I be confident." Or when he said, "God is our hope and strength, a help in trouble ready to be found: therefore will not we fear, though the earth be moved, though the mountains be hurled into the depth of the sea," he would not have so despaired in these and like circumstances.

Had Abraham had the same understanding of God when he feigned his wife to be his sister as when God promised to give him a son and when he went to sacrifice his son, he could have trusted and depended on God in this case as well as in the former, this difficulty being far less than the other.

If God's people could see God at all times as they saw him at some times, they would be better able to depend on him and trust in him *no matter what* comes their way. But if they lose their spiritual sight and conception of God by faith, they shall never be able to believe and depend upon God in any difficulty.

We should also beware of forgetting his former works. In Psalm 78:6-7, the people were commanded to tell the wondrous works of God to their children, that the generations to come might set their hope in God and not forget the works of God. This confirms that the best way to maintain their hope and dependance on God was to hold up the remembrance of what he had done. He that forgets the one will not be able to do the other.

It is true that forgetting God's former mercies causes us to distrust and hinders us in our dependence on God for present and future straits. And to the contrary, holding up the remembrance of former mercies enables us to be strong in present and future distresses.

You cannot think his arm is shortened. You cannot think God cannot, nor can you think God will not. You must not believe that even though he has helped before, he will help no more. For mercy is tied to the church by covenant.

Wicked men may enjoy a mercy today, but they can have no assurance that they will have another tomorrow because mercy is not tied to them by *promise* or by *covenant*. But mercy is tied to the church by covenant, by promise. He has tied his mercy to us by his truth.

God performs his promises, and we may therefore challenge his mercy by virtue of his truth. This is the reason David could say in Psalm 23:6, "Surely mercy and goodness shall follow me all the days of my life." Not in this or that instance, but in every passage of providence. Just as the water followed the children of Israel, so did the rock (1 Cor. 10:4).

Because God does wonders for his church, it is good to be a member of his body, his church. Though our enemies have skill, power, strength, and numbers, we have a God who is stronger than the strongest, wiser than the wisest, who can both overpower and out-plot our enemies. Our God alone can do wonders for us. Whatever you may be lacking, if you have God, you have everything and more that you need. So do not be discouraged when your adversaries glory in their strength, their skill, their power, and their numbers, for you have God and his truth, and he can do wonders for you.

When Christ did that great wonder in calming the raging sea, the text tells us, "They all fell down at the feet of Jesus and worshipped him." Even a heathen king, when he saw the wonders God had done, said "Let all men fear and tremble before the God of Daniel," (Dan. 6:26). Fall down then, at the feet of God and worship him. Fall down at the feet of his power and dread it. Fall down at the feet of his mercy and adore it. Fall down at the feet of his wisdom and admire it.

Because God does wonders for his church, let us carry ourselves in a fashion suitable to such, expecting that God will do wonders for us. Oh, that we could put ourselves in a posture suitable for mercy and deliverance! "Seeing you look for a new heaven and a new earth, wherein dwells righteousness, what manner of persons ought you to be?" If you expect that God will do wonders for you, what kind of person should you be in holiness of life? How spiritual ought you to be in all manner of conversation and behavior! See that you do not sin in the face of mercy, in the face of deliverance as Israel did, provoking God at the Red Sea (Ps. 106:7).

Nothing but our sin hinders the current and stream of his mercy. As in Jeremiah 18:9-10, "At what time I shall speak concerning a nation, or a kingdom, to build and to plant it: if they do evil in my sight, and do not obey my voice, then I will repent of the good wherewith I said, I would benefit them." Our sins put obstructions in the way of all God's proceedings of mercy.

And therefore you see, when the temple was to be built and great things were to be done for them, the prophet by way of necessary preparation, exhorts the people to repentance, to cast away their sins (Haggai 1:6). Knowing this, that though God had begun to show mercy, if they continued in their sins, they would have quickly stopped God's mercy and God would have soon repented of his mercy to them.

God brought Israel out of Egypt and near Canaan. Yet their sins came between them and Canaan, causing them to turn back again to the wilderness where they walked in a circle for forty years before they could find admission into Canaan.

God has gone out before us, triumphing in the greatness of his strength, preparing a way, knocking down difficulties, leveling mountains, turning all our oppositions into good. But if you do not leave your sins, you will make God quickly leave you.

But because you are all expectants of his mercy, let every one of you labor to put himself into a posture worthy to receive mercy. Let everyone walk as those who look for great things from God, and then that God that has begun his work in you will certainly complete it. He that has laid the foundation, and is laying stone after stone upon it every day, will not desist until the building be perfected.

Because God does wonders for his church, we should trust in him. As Christ said in Mark 9:23, "If you can believe, all things are possible to him that believes." There is nothing too hard for God to do, if there is nothing too hard for you to believe. There is nothing for you to do but believe. He that has conquered and overcome his own unbelief has done all. All things are possible to the believer. By faith they subdued kingdoms, stopped the mouths of lions, quenched the violence of fire, *etc.* (Heb. 11:33-34). As unbelief imprisons God's power, mercy, and goodness, it is said that "he could not do much, because of their unbelief." Unbelief limits the holy one of Israel.

Likewise, faith sets God and his power at liberty. Therefore, exercise faith. The time of our trouble should be the time of our trust. As Mordecai said about Esther, God set her up for such a time, so I may say of faith: God set up faith for such a time as this. When means fail, when there is nothing but weakness below, when sense and reason are lacking, then is it faith that comes to work. Therefore, exercise faith.

Do not allow any difficulty to undermine faith. Do not let any seeming discouragement come between your souls and the promise.

Things marvelous to you are familiar with God; things wonderful to you are easy to God. In God's word you find that all things are possible with God; therefore, nothing is impossible to faith.

Be encouraged to pray. Faith coupled with prayer will do wonders. Faith and prayer have had a hand in most of the wonders that were ever done in the earth. These two will set the great God on doing wonders for us. A prayer made up of promises, lifted heavenward by faith, will show wonders in heaven and in earth.

You read of what wonders God's people have wrought by prayer. They dried up the sea (Exod. 14:21), brought down fire from heaven (2 Kings 1:10), caused the sun to stand still (Josh. 10:13), and vanquished the enemy (Exod. 17:12).

See what wonders followed David's prayer in Psalm 18:6, "In my distress I called upon the Lord, I cried to my God. He heard my voice out of his temple, my cry came unto his ears." And then we see in verses 7-8, 13-14, "Then the earth shook and trembled: the Lord thundered in the heavens and the highest gave his voice, hailstones, and coals of fire. He sent out his arrows, and scattered them, he shot out his lightnings, and discomfited them."

When trouble and evil threaten and the enemy comes like a flood irresistibly, then the Spirit of the Lord shall go up against them. He will be your defense and chase them away (Isa. 54:15).

When God intends to bestow great things on his people, he first gives them the spirit of prayer, the forerunner of mercy (Jer. 3:19). So be encouraged to hope as well as to pray. In Hebrews 6:19, hope is called "the anchor of the soul, sure and steadfast." God delights in those who hope in his mercy (Ps. 147:11). And whom God delights in, enemies shall not delight over. Hope is the daughter of faith, so when faith gives birth to prayer, let it also bring forth hope.

We should also be encouraged to *wait*, for as long as we hope we will wait, and no longer. If you expect and hope your friend will come to you, you will stay and wait for him. Hope both expects that mercy will come, and then it waits until it does come. This kind of hope is confident of God's goodness and truth, that in due time he will show mercy. It is conscious of its own duty, and therefore humbly and patiently waits for God's time, for they know by experience that the Lord is good to them that wait for him, to the soul that seeks him (Lam. 3:25).

And when you have learned these lessons of trusting in God, praying, hoping, and waiting on him, then you shall say with the prophet in Isaiah 25:9, "Lo, this is our God; we have waited for him, and he will save us. This is the Lord; we have waited for him; we will rejoice and be joyful in his salvation."

If you will engage God to do wonders, you must first believe he will. Allow faith to have her full and perfect work. There is no temptation so powerful that faith cannot conquer, no affliction so great that faith cannot master, no prison so strong that faith cannot open, no danger so fierce that faith cannot rescue, no misery so unsufferable that faith cannot deliver us from. As Christ said, "believe, and you shall see the wondrous works of God." It is as if he had said, "God will do no wonders if you do not believe," for Christ himself said he did not do "many works there because of their unbelief," (Matt. 13:58).

Unbelief takes no power nor wisdom from God, as the apostle said, "God is faithful whether men believe or not." Yet our unbelief robs us of all. Though he has mercy, he has none for us. So, our first charge is to believe that our God is a God of power, and this God and this power is yours because of the covenant. Let faith now awaken then, because if you can believe, all wonders are possible. As Mark 9:23 says, "If you can believe, all things are possible to him who believes." To believe is difficult; but to him that believes, nothing is impossible. "If you have faith as a grain of mustard seed and say to this mountain, 'be removed from here and be cast into the sea,' it shall be done," (Matt. 17:20). That is, whatever may be to the glory of God and the good of his church, no matter how difficult, even the least faith, if true faith, will bring it about. Hebrews 11:33 tells us of the many wonders faith brought about, and we have the same power and the same God available to us today.

Resolve to give God no rest until he has established Zion, the joy and praise of the whole earth. God has a larger heart to give than you have to ask. He will allow no one to equal him in his love for his church. As Ephesians 3:20 states, "He is able to do exceedingly abundantly above all that we are able to ask or think," and Jeremiah 33:3 says, "Call unto me, and I will answer you and show you great and mighty things, which you do not know."

Knowing these promises, allow no difficulty to undermine your faith nor discouragement to put you off from seeking. Jacob persisted in prayer, notwithstanding all his discouragements. Though he wrestled in the night, though he was all alone, though God smote him in his thigh, yet he held out to wrestle with God.

If you would prevail with God, you must not only pray, but *continue* in prayer. Jacob prayed all night, David day and night, Jonah three days and three nights, Daniel 21 days and 21 nights, Moses 40 days and 40 nights. No matter if God delays, defers, or denies, still persist in prayer. Urge God with his own promises, with his glory, with his name, with his truth, with his worship, *etc.*, for all of these are precious to him.

There is nothing too hard for that people to do whose hearts and spirits God mightily upholds to seek him. Further, you know what wonders prayer has done. Prayer has been the great engine that carries out all God's purposes. Nothing has been done without it, and nothing has been done against it. When sin drew the sword, prayer sheathed it again. When sin covered us with a cloud of blood, prayer dispelled and scattered it. Glory be to God. And you who have experienced this, be encouraged to it again. Be mighty with God and faith, and prayer will work wonders.

Finally, to be mighty in prayer you must give heed to your reformation. *Supplication is nothing without reformation.* As Isaiah 59:1-2 states, "The arm of the Lord is not shortened that he cannot save, nor is his ear heavy that he cannot hear. But your iniquities have separated between you and your God, and your sins have hidden his face from you, that he will not hear." It is as if the prophet had said, "God is as powerful, and as merciful as he ever was. He is as able to do wonders, and as willing as he ever was. But the reason he does not do them is because of your sin. Your sin robs you of his goodness." You look upward to see whether God will help. You look downward to see whether man can help. But what is all this if you do not look inward to see your sins which hinder God's help and cast them away. Judges 10:10-12 tells us that God often delivered Israel, and they now found themselves again in new distresses. They cry out to God, but God tells them because they had walked unworthy of former deliverances, he would deliver them no more. On hearing these words, they go and confess their sins before God, they humble themselves before him and reform their evil ways. And then, said the text, "his soul was grieved for their misery," and God delivered them again.

Let us go and humble ourselves and seek God's forgiveness, else God's soul may not be grieved for our miseries. Then when God sees us reform, we trust he will be merciful to our souls. When he sees us grieved for our sins, he will then be grieved for our miseries.

Reform your families, your churches, your person. Set yourself to do the work of reformation, and God will not fail to do wonders for you.

God is intent on the great design of his own glory. We are wise to take notice of it, to further it and not hinder it.

See that you reform your pride, your lukewarmness, your covetousness, your vanities, your unthankfulness, your unfruitfulness, and your lack of love for the brethren.

For when God sees us repent in a posture of reformation, he will preserve us. He will do wonders for his people!

FINIS

Other Helpful Works Published by Puritan Publications

A Devotional on Our Savior's Death and Passion
by Charles Herle (1598-1659)

Herle's masterful devotional forms each chapter into a respective day's meditation. In his work, there are 41 devotionals on the passion and death of Christ, with a concluding meditation on the resurrection; that Christ is a dying and rising Savior.

The Wonders of Jesus
by Jeremiah Burroughs (1599-1646)

Christ is wonderful in his offices, miracles, and in regard to the glory of the Father that shines in him. This great wonder is little known in the world.

The Great Mystery of God's Providence, and Other Works
by George Gifford (1547-1620)

This particular work by Gifford contains six pieces now updated into current modern print. His work on providence is worth the cost of the volume alone.

A Biblical Guide to Hearing and Studying the Word
by Richard Greenham, et. al.

What Christian does not desire to improve their ability to hear the word of God preached with profit, and to study the word of God with profit? This puritan compilation is a tool not to be missed!

The Sweetness of Divine Meditation
by William Bridge (1600-1670)

It is meditation that makes you master of the truths that you read or hear; otherwise, the wisdom remains in the book – *William Bridge.*

www.ingramcontent.com/pod-product-compliance
Lightning Source LLC
Chambersburg PA
CBHW030851090426
42737CB00009B/1194